6/08

JELLYFISH

PowerKiDS
press.
New York

Published in 2008 by The Rosen Publishing Group, Inc.
29 East 21st Street, New York, NY 10010

First Edition

Editor: Jennifer Way
Book Design: Kate Laczynski
Photo Researcher: Nicole Pristash

Photo Credits: All images © Shutterstock.com.

Library of Congress Cataloging-in-Publication Data

McFee, Shane.
 Jellyfish / Shane McFee. — 1st ed.
    p. cm. — (Poison!)
 Includes bibliographical references and index.
 ISBN-13: 978-1-4042-3799-5 (library binding)
 ISBN-10: 1-4042-3799-2 (library binding)
 1. Jellyfishes—Juvenile literature. I. Title.
 QL377.S4M34 2008
 593.5'3—dc22

                                    2007000565

Manufactured in the United States of America

CONTENTS

JELLYFISH

You may have seen jellyfish on the beach. Sometimes there are signs on the beach that tell you to watch out for jellyfish.

Jellyfish live in every ocean in the world. They are known for their painful **stings**. Some jellyfish sting with venom, or poison, that is deadly to people. There are more than 2,000 different kinds of jellyfish. Only 70 of these can hurt humans. This book will tell you about the deadliest jellyfish and what to do if you are stung by one.

This is an Australian spotted jellyfish. These jellyfish live in the South Pacific Ocean. A sting from this jellyfish will hurt, but it will not be deadly.

NO BRAINS

Jellyfish are not really fish at all. They are cnidarians. Cnidarians are very simple **organisms**. This means that a jellyfish body does not have the same kinds of organs, or body parts, that other animals have.

Jellyfish do not have **brains**, hearts, or bones. Most of them do not even have eyes. They do not see, but they can sense light with tiny hairs called **cilia**. Their skin is so thin that they can breathe through it!

Jellyfish are very slow swimmers. They generally just float on the water.

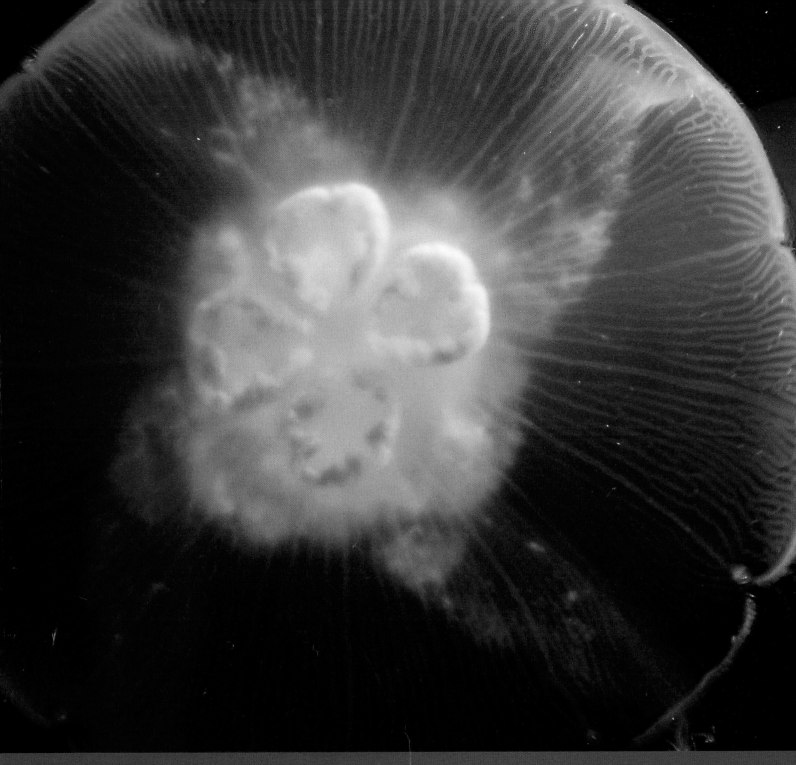

This is the underside of a jellyfish's body. The space in the very center is its mouth. The mouth is surrounded by all its other body parts.

WHAT DO JELLYFISH LOOK LIKE?

Jellyfish look a little like floating mushrooms. The part of the jellyfish that looks like the top of a mushroom is called the bell. Most jellyfish have long **tentacles** and oral arms, which float in the water below the bell.

Different kinds of jellyfish are different colors. They can be orange, red, purple, green, yellow, blue, or white. Sometimes they have stripes. The bright colors warn other ocean animals to stay away. The skin of jellyfish is so thin that light passes through it.

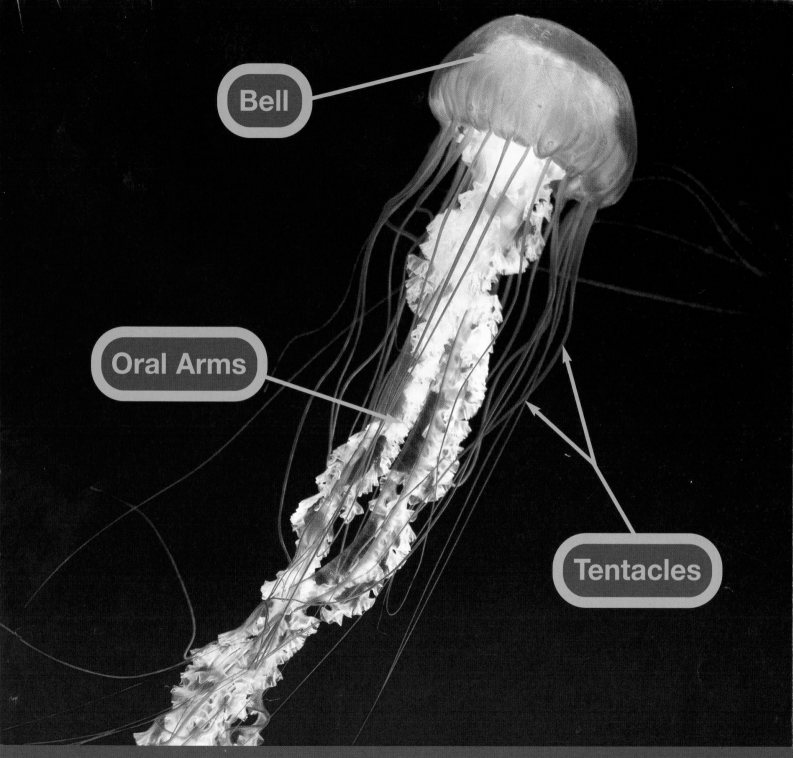

Bell

Oral Arms

Tentacles

This moon jellyfish has been labeled to show its bell, its tentacles, and its oral arms. The oral arms are used to move food that has been caught in the tentacles to the mouth.

FOOD

Most jellyfish eat small fish and **zooplankton**. Zooplankton are tiny organisms. Even though they eat other animals, jellyfish do not hunt for them. They wait for something to swim into their tentacles. They sting anything that touches them. The sting will kill or **paralyze** small animals. Then the jellyfish will use its tentacles to pull the animal into its mouth.

The jellyfish also uses its sting to fight off larger animals. Some fish and sea turtles eat jellyfish. The stings do not hurt these animals.

Jellyfish will eat small fish that swim into their tentacles and use their sting to fight off larger fish. Inset: Some kinds of sea turtles are not hurt by jellyfish stings and will hunt and eat jellyfish.

HOW DO JELLYFISH STING?

Jellyfish use their tentacles to sting. Each tentacle is covered with **nematocysts**. Nematocysts have triggers and sharp barbs, which give the sting. When an animal runs into a tentacle, it sets off the trigger. The trigger tells the sharp barbs to stick the animal. The barbs **inject** venom into the animal. One tentacle can have thousands of nematocysts. That means the tentacle can have thousands of barbs.

Jellyfish never attack people. People are stung only if they touch a jellyfish's tentacle. This can happen while swimming or walking barefoot on the beach.

Each of this jellyfish's tentacles is full of thousands of nematocysts, which can inject venom into an unlucky swimmer.

REPRODUCTION

Jellyfish do not reproduce, or make babies, in the same way that other animals do. Unlike most other animals, the male jellyfish does not need to touch the female jellyfish in order to **fertilize** her eggs! A male jellyfish lets out his **sperm** into the water. The sperm then floats toward the female jellyfish's body, where her eggs are.

Female jellyfish hold the eggs in their tentacles. When the sperm floats past the tentacles, the eggs can be fertilized. When they hatch, or come out of their eggs, baby jellyfish are known as **larvae**.

When jellyfish prepare to reproduce, they need only to be floating near each other. After the eggs are fertilized, most jellyfish females hold the eggs in their mouth until the larvae are ready to hatch. 15

POLYPS AND MEDUSAE

Most jellyfish have two basic life stages. They are called **polyps** during their first stage of life. Polyps grow on rocks and coral. They are shaped like cups and have very small tentacles. Polyps do not look like animals at all. They look like plants. In fact, they grow by making buds, like plants.

The polyp will bud off a young jellyfish. The jellyfish will then grow into a **medusa**. This is the second stage of life. The medusa is a full-grown adult jellyfish.

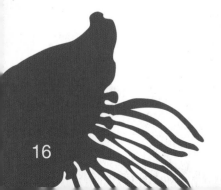

When polyps bud off a young jellyfish, like the ones here, they are called ephyra. Ephyra will soon grow into the medusa, or adult stage. Most jellyfish live about six months.

17

THE BOX JELLYFISH

The box jellyfish is the deadliest jellyfish in the ocean. Most box jellyfish live in the waters near Australia. The box jellyfish got its name because the bell is shaped like a box. This jellyfish is also known as the sea wasp.

The venom of the box jellyfish is very powerful. Once the tentacles sting, they do not let go. Removing the tentacles sometimes causes even more stings. Some scientists believe box jellyfish are deadlier than sharks.

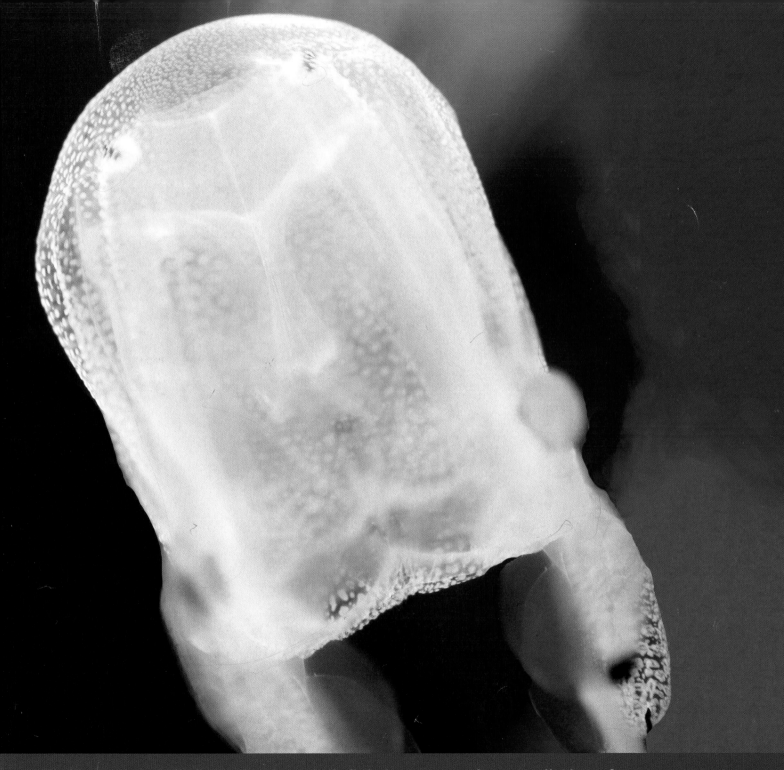

Unlike other jellyfish, the box jellyfish has eyes. It actually has four groups of them!

THE PORTUGUESE MAN-OF-WAR

The Portuguese man-of-war is often mistaken for a jellyfish. Like jellyfish, it is a cnidarian, but it is actually a grouping of polyps.

The Portuguese man-of-war uses an organ called an air bladder. The air bladder lets it float and control the direction in which it moves, like a boat's sail does.

The Portuguese man-of-war's tentacles drift under the air bladder. The tentacles are around 30 feet (10 m) long. This means that you can get stung when you are not near this animal! A man-of-war sting is painful but not deadly. However, in some cases people have died from the venomous stings.

The Portuguese man-of-war keeps its bladder wet by rolling over. It can let gas out so it can sink and hide from its enemies.

WHAT SHOULD YOU DO?

What should you do if you get one of these painful stings? First, you should put **vinegar** or salt water on jellyfish stings. Do not rub the sting. Some people think you should use rubbing alcohol on jellyfish stings. They are wrong. This will make the sting worse.

If you are stung on the beach, try to find a lifeguard. If you are stung by a box jellyfish, you should see a doctor.

If you see a jellyfish, leave it alone. Its sting is very painful. If you are on the beach, look out for dead jellyfish. Even dead jellyfish can sting!

GLOSSARY

brains (BRAYNZ) The soft body parts found in the head that allow thought, movement, and feeling.

cilia (SIH-lee-ah) Tiny hairs.

fertilize (FUR-tuh-lyz) To put male cells inside an egg to make babies.

inject (in-JEKT) To use a sharp object to force something into a body.

larvae (LAHR-vee) Animals in the early life stage in which they have a wormlike form.

medusa (mih-DOO-suh) The adult stage of a jellyfish.

nematocysts (NEH-muh-tuh-sists) The stingers of some types of animals.

organisms (OR-guh-nih-zumz) Living beings made of dependent parts.

paralyze (PER-uh-lyz) To take away feeling or movement in the limbs.

polyps (PAH-lips) The first stage of a jellyfish's life.

sperm (SPERM) A special male cell that, with a female egg, can make a baby.

stings (STINGZ) Pains caused by animals using a sharp part to hurt another animal.

tentacles (TEN-tih-kulz) Long, thin growths on animals that are used to touch, hold, or move.

vinegar (VIH-nih-ger) A sour liquid used in cooking.

zooplankton (zoh-uh-PLANK-tun) Tiny animals that float freely in water.

INDEX

WEB SITES

Due to the changing nature of Internet links, PowerKids Press has developed an online list of Web sites related to the subject of this book. This site is updated regularly. Please use this link to access the list:
www.powerkidslinks.com/poi/jelly/